Trace and Write Bible Passages & Verses

Cursive Handwriting Practice

Over 5,500 cursive tracing units.

* Ten Commandments
* 23rd Psalm
* Beatitudes
* Whole Armor of God

Macy McCullough

Book A

Trace the Bible verse. Then rewrite the verse on the blank lines below.

And God spake all these words, saying, I am the Lord thy God, which have brought thee out of the land of Egypt, out of the house of bondage.

Trace the Bible verse. Then rewrite the verse on the blank lines below.

Thou shalt have no other gods before me. Thou shalt not make unto thee any graven image, or any likeness of any thing that is in heaven above,

Trace the Bible verse. Then rewrite the verse on the blank lines below.

or that is in the earth beneath, or that is in the water under the earth. shalt not bow down thyself to them, nor serve them: for I the Lord thy God am a

Trace the Bible verse. Then rewrite the verse on the blank lines below.

jealous God, visiting the
iniquity of the fathers upon
the children unto the third
and fourth generation of
them that hate me; And
shewing mercy unto

Trace the Bible verse. Then rewrite the verse on the blank lines below.

thousands of them that love me, and keep my commandments. Thou not take the name of the Lord thy God in vain; for the Lord will not hold him

Trace the Bible verse. Then rewrite the verse on the blank lines below.

guiltless that taketh his name in vain. Remember the sabbath day, to keep it holy. Six days shalt thou labour, and do all thy work: But seventh day is

Trace the Bible verse. Then rewrite the verse on the blank lines below.

the sabbath of the Lord thy God: in it thou shalt not do any work, thou, nor thy son, nor thy daughter thy manservant, nor thy maidservant, nor thy

Trace the Bible verse. Then rewrite the verse on the blank lines below.

nor thy stranger that is within thy gates: For in six days the Lord made heaven and earth, the sea, and all that in them is, and rested the seventh day: wherefore

Trace the Bible verse. Then rewrite the verse on the blank lines below.

the Lord blessed the sabbath day, and hallowed it. Honour thy father and thy mother: that thy days may be long upon the land which the Lord thy God

Trace the Bible verse. Then rewrite the verse on the blank lines below.

giveth thee. Thou shalt not kill. Thou shalt not commit adultery. Thou shalt not steal. Thou shalt not bear false witness against thy neighbor.

Trace the Bible verse. Then rewrite the verse on the blank lines below.

Thou shalt not covet thy neighbour's house, thou shalt not covet thy neighbour's wife, nor his manservant, nor his maidservant, nor his ox,

Trace the Bible verse. Then rewrite the verse on the blank lines below.

nor his ass, nor any thing that is in thy neighbour's.
Exodus 20:1-17
King James Version

Bible Facts

Trace the bible facts below.

The Old Testament has 17
historical books in it:
Genesis, Exodus, Leviticus,
Numbers, Deuteronomy
Joshua, Judges, Ruth,
1 Samuel, 2 Samuel
1 Kings, 2 Kings,
1 Chronicles, 2 Chronicles
Ezra, Nehemiah, and Esther.

23rd Psalm

Trace the Bible verse. Then rewrite the verse on the blank lines below.

The Lord is my shepherd; I shall not want. He maketh me to lie down in green pastures: he leadeth me beside the still waters. He restoreth my soul: he leadeth

Trace the Bible verse. Then rewrite the verse on the blank lines below.

me in the paths of righteousness for his name's sake. Yea though I walk through the valley of the shadow of death, I will fear no evil: for thou art with

Trace the Bible verse. Then rewrite the verse on the blank lines below.

me; thy rod and thy staff they comfort me. Thou preparest a table before me in the presence of mine enemies: thou anointest my head with oil; my cup runneth

Trace the Bible verse. Then rewrite the verse on the blank lines below.

over. Surely goodness and mercy shall follow me all the days of my life: and I will dwell in the house of the Lord for ever. Psalm 23 King James Version

Bible Facts

Trace the bible facts below.

The Old Testament has 17 prophetic books in it: Isaiah, Lamentations, Jeremiah, Ezekiel, Daniel Hosea, Joel, Amos, Obadiah Jonah, Micah, Nahum, Habakkuk, Zephaniah Haggai, Zechariah, and Malachi

Beatitudes

Trace the Bible verse. Then rewrite the verse on the blank lines below.

And seeing the multitudes, He went up into a mountain: and when He was set, His disciples came unto Him: and He opened His mouth, and taught

Trace the Bible verse. Then rewrite the verse on the blank lines below.

them, saying, Blessed are the poor in spirit: for theirs is the kingdom of heaven. Blessed are they that mourn: for they shall be comforted. Blessed are the meek: for

Trace and Write: Bible Passages & Verses

Trace the Bible verse. Then rewrite the verse on the blank lines below.

they shall inherit the earth. Blessed are they which do hunger and thirst after righteousness: for they shall be filled. Blessed are the merciful: for they shall

Trace the Bible verse. Then rewrite the verse on the blank lines below.

obtain mercy. Blessed are the pure in heart: for they shall see God. Blessed are the peacemakers: for they shall be called the children of God. Blessed are they which are

Trace the Bible verse. Then rewrite the verse on the blank lines below.

persecuted for righteousness'
sake: for theirs is the
kingdom of heaven. Blessed
are ye, when men shall
revile you, and persecute
you, and shall say all

Trace the Bible verse. Then rewrite the verse on the blank lines below.

manner of evil against you falsely, for my sake. Rejoice and be exceeding glad: for great is your reward in heaven: for so persecuted they the prophets which

Trace the Bible verse. Then rewrite the verse on the blank lines below.

were before you.

Matthew 5:1-12

King James Version

Whole Armor of God

Trace the Bible verse. Then rewrite the verse on the blank lines below.

Finally, my brethren, be strong in the Lord, and in the power of his might. Put on the whole armour of God, that ye may be able to stand against the wiles

Trace and Write: Bible Passages & Verses

Trace the Bible verse. Then rewrite the verse on the blank lines below.

of the devil. For we wrestle

not against flesh and blood,

but against principalities,

and powers, against the

rulers of the darkness of

this world, against

Trace the Bible verse. Then rewrite the verse on the blank lines below.

spiritual wickedness in high places. Wherefore take unto you the whole armour of God, that ye may be able to withstand in the evil day, and have done all, to stand.

Trace the Bible verse. Then rewrite the verse on the blank lines below.

Stand therefore, having your loins girt about with truth, and having on the breastplate of righteousness; And your feet shod with the preparation of the gospel of

Trace the Bible verse. Then rewrite the verse on the blank lines below.

peace; Above all, taking the shield of faith, wherewith ye shall be able to quench all the fiery darts of the wicked. And take the helmet of salvation, and the sword

Trace the Bible verse. Then rewrite the verse on the blank lines below.

of the Spirit, which is the word of God: Praying always with all prayer and supplication in the Spirit, and watching thereunto with all perseverance and

Trace the Bible verse. Then rewrite the verse on the blank lines below.

supplication for all saints

Ephesians 6:10-18

King James Version

Alphabet Practice

Trace the letter Aa. Then write the letter Aa as many times as possible.

A a   Abraham

A A A

A A A

A A A

A A A

A A A

A A A

a a a

a a a

a a a

a a a

a a a

Trace and Write: Bible Passages & Verses

Trace the letter Aa. Then write the letter Aa as many times as possible.

A a   Adam

A A A

A A A

A A A

A A A

A A A

A A A

a a a

a a a

a a a

a a a

a a a

Trace the letter Aa. Then write the letter Aa as many times as possible.

A a Accusation

A A A

A A A

A A A

A A A

A A A

A A A

a a a

a a a

a a a

a a a

a a a

Trace the letter Bb. Then write the letter Bb as many times as possible.

B b Bethlehem

Trace the letter Bb. Then write the letter Bb as many times as possible.

B b Bagpipe

Trace the letter Bb. Then write the letter Bb as many times as possible.

Bb Balances

B B B

B B B

B B B

B B B

B B B

B B B

b b b

b b b

b b b

b b b

b b b

Trace the letter Cc. Then write the letter Cc as many times as possible.

C c Canaan

Trace and Write: Bible Passages & Verses

Trace the letter Cc. Then write the letter Cc as many times as possible.

C c Candlestick

C C C

C C C

C C C

C C C

C C C

C C C

c c c

c c c

c c c

c c c

c c c

Trace and Write: Bible Passages & Verses

Trace the letter Cc. Then write the letter Cc as many times as possible.

C c   Captain

Trace the letter Dd. Then write the letter Dd as many times as possible.

D d Damascus

D D D

D D D

D D D

D D D

D D D

D D D

d d d

d d d

d d d

d d d

d d d

Trace the letter Dd. Then write the letter Dd as many times as possible.

D d   Daniel

D D D

D D D

D D D

D D D

D D D

D D D

d d d

d d d

d d d

d d d

d d d

Trace the letter Dd. Then write the letter Dd as many times as possible.

D d   Daughter

Trace and Write: Bible Passages & Verses

Trace the letter Ee. Then write the letter Ee as many times as possible.

E e Earthquake

E   E   E

E   E   E

E   E   E

E   E   E

E   E   E

E   E   E

e   e   e

e   e   e

e   e   e

e   e   e

e   e   e

Trace and Write: Bible Passages & Verses

Trace the letter Ee. Then write the letter Ee as many times as possible.

E e   Ebenezer

Trace the letter Ee. Then write the letter Ee as many times as possible.

E e Ebony

E E E

E E E

E E E

E E E

E E E

E E E

e e e

e e e

e e e

e e e

e e e

Trace and Write: Bible Passages & Verses

Trace the letter Ff. Then write the letter Ff as many times as possible.

Ff   Fasting

F F F

F F F

F F F

F F F

F F F

F F F

f f f

f f f

f f f

f f f

f f f

Trace and Write: Bible Passages & Verses

Trace the letter Ff. Then write the letter Ff as many times as possible.

Ff Family

Trace and Write: Bible Passages & Verses

Trace the letter Ff. Then write the letter Ff as many times as possible.

Ff Festivals

F F F

F F F

F F F

F F F

F F F

F F F

f f f

f f f

f f f

f f f

f f f

Trace and Write: Bible Passages & Verses

Trace the letter Gg. Then write the letter Gg as many times as possible.

G g   Genealogy

Trace the letter Gg. Then write the letter Gg as many times as possible.

G g Gather

Trace and Write: Bible Passages & Verses

Trace the letter Gg. Then write the letter Gg as many times as possible.

G g   Gentiles

Trace the letter Hh. Then write the letter Hh as many times as possible.

H h Habakkuk

Trace and Write: Bible Passages & Verses

Trace the letter Hh. Then write the letter Hh as many times as possible.

H h Hammer

H H H

H H H

H H H

H H H

H H H

H H H

h h h

h h h

h h h

h h h

h h h

Trace the letter Hh. Then write the letter Hh as many times as possible.

H h Harvest

H H H

H H H

H H H

H H H

H H H

H H H

h h h

h h h

h h h

h h h

h h h

Trace and Write: Bible Passages & Verses

Trace the letter Ii. Then write the letter Ii as many times as possible.

Ii Image

Trace the letter Ii. Then write the letter Ii as many times as possible.

Ii Insects

Trace and Write: Bible Passages & Verses

Trace the letter Ii. Then write the letter Ii as many times as possible.

Ii Isaac

I I I

I I I

I I I

I I I

I I I

I I I

i i i

i i i

i i i

i i i

i i i

Trace and Write: Bible Passages & Verses

Trace the letter Jj. Then write the letter Jj as many times as possible.

J j Jabez

Trace and Write: Bible Passages & Verses

Trace the letter Jj. Then write the letter Jj as many times as possible.

J j James

Trace and Write: Bible Passages & Verses

Trace the letter Jj. Then write the letter Jj as many times as possible.

J j Jesus

Trace the letter Kk. Then write the letter Kk as many times as possible.

Kk Key

Trace the letter Kk. Then write the letter Kk as many times as possible.

Kk   Kindness

Trace and Write: Bible Passages & Verses

Trace the letter Kk. Then write the letter Kk as many times as possible.

Kk Kingdom

K K K

K K K

K K K

K K K

K K K

K K K

k k k

k k k

k k k

k k k

k k k

Trace and Write: Bible Passages & Verses

Trace the letter Ll. Then write the letter Ll as many times as possible.

L l Ladder

L L L

L L L

L L L

L L L

L L L

L L L

l l l

l l l

l l l

l l l

l l l

Trace and Write: Bible Passages & Verses

Trace the letter Ll. Then write the letter Ll as many times as possible.

L l Language

Trace the letter Ll. Then write the letter Ll as many times as possible.

L l Laughter

L L L

L L L

L L L

L L L

L L L

L L L

l l l

l l l

l l l

l l l

l l l

Trace and Write: Bible Passages & Verses

Trace the letter Mm. Then write the letter Mm as many times as possible.

M m Mammon

Trace and Write: Bible Passages & Verses

Trace the letter Mm. Then write the letter Mm as many times as possible.

M m   Mandrake

Trace and Write: Bible Passages & Verses

Trace the letter Mm. Then write the letter Mm as many times as possible.

M m   Mantle

m m m

m m m

m m m

m m m

m m m

m m m

m m m

m m m

m m m

m m m

m m m

Trace and Write: Bible Passages & Verses

Trace the letter Nn. Then write the letter Nn as many times as possible.

N n Nazereth

n n n

n n n

n n n

n n n

n n n

n n n

n n n

n n n

n n n

n n n

n n n

Trace the letter Nn. Then write the letter Nn as many times as possible.

N n Nehemiah

Trace and Write: Bible Passages & Verses

Trace the letter Nn. Then write the letter Nn as many times as possible.

N n   Neighbor

Trace and Write: Bible Passages & Verses

Trace the letter Oo. Then write the letter Oo as many times as possible.

O o   Oath

Trace the letter Oo. Then write the letter Oo as many times as possible.

Oo Obadiah

Trace and Write: Bible Passages & Verses

Trace the letter Oo. Then write the letter Oo as many times as possible.

Oo Offering

Trace the letter Pp. Then write the letter Pp as many times as possible.

P p   Palestine

P P P

P P P

P P P

P P P

P P P

P P P

p p p

p p p

p p p

p p p

p p p

Trace and Write: Bible Passages & Verses

Trace the letter Pp. Then write the letter Pp as many times as possible.

P p   Papyrus

Trace the letter Pp. Then write the letter Pp as many times as possible.

P p   Parable

P P P

P P P

P P P

P P P

P P P

P P P

p p p

p p p

p p p

p p p

p p p

Trace and Write: Bible Passages & Verses

Trace the letter Qq. Then write the letter Qq as many times as possible.

Q q   Quail

Trace the letter Qq. Then write the letter Qq as many times as possible.

Q q Quiver

Trace and Write: Bible Passages & Verses

Trace the letter Qq. Then write the letter Qq as many times as possible.

Q q   Queen

Trace and Write: Bible Passages & Verses

Trace the letter Rr. Then write the letter Rr as many times as possible.

R r Rabbi

R R R

R R R

R R R

R R R

R R R

R R R

r r r

r r r

r r r

r r r

r r r

Trace the letter Rr. Then write the letter Rr as many times as possible.

Rr Raiment

Trace the letter Rr. Then write the letter Rr as many times as possible.

R r   Refuge

Trace the letter Ss. Then write the letter Ss as many times as possible.

Ss Sabbath

Trace the letter Ss. Then write the letter Ss as many times as possible.

S s   Salvation

Trace and Write: Bible Passages & Verses

Trace the letter Ss. Then write the letter Ss as many times as possible.

Ss Samuel

Trace the letter Tt. Then write the letter Tt as many times as possible.

Tt Tapestry

Trace and Write: Bible Passages & Verses

Trace the letter Tt. Then write the letter Tt as many times as possible.

Tt Teacher

Trace and Write: Bible Passages & Verses

Trace the letter Tt. Then write the letter Tt as many times as possible.

Tt   Temple

Trace and Write: Bible Passages & Verses

Trace the letter Uu. Then write the letter Uu as many times as possible.

Uu Unclean

U U U

U U U

U U U

U U U

U U U

U U U

u u u

u u u

u u u

u u u

u u u

Trace and Write: Bible Passages & Verses

Trace the letter Uu. Then write the letter Uu as many times as possible.

Uu Upright

Trace and Write: Bible Passages & Verses

Trace the letter Uu. Then write the letter Uu as many times as possible.

Uu Usury

𝒰 𝒰 𝒰

𝒰 𝒰 𝒰

𝒰 𝒰 𝒰

𝒰 𝒰 𝒰

𝒰 𝒰 𝒰

𝒰 𝒰 𝒰

𝓊 𝓊 𝓊

𝓊 𝓊 𝓊

𝓊 𝓊 𝓊

𝓊 𝓊 𝓊

𝓊 𝓊 𝓊

Trace the letter Vv. Then write the letter Vv as many times as possible.

V v Victory

Trace and Write: Bible Passages & Verses

Trace the letter Vv. Then write the letter Vv as many times as possible.

V v   Vineyard

Trace and Write: Bible Passages & Verses

Trace the letter Vv. Then write the letter Vv as many times as possible.

V v Virtue

Trace and Write: Bible Passages & Verses

Trace the letter Ww. Then write the letter Ww as many times as possible.

W w Watchman

W W W

W W W

W W W

W W W

W W W

W W W

w w w

w w w

w w w

w w w

w w w

w w w

Trace and Write: Bible Passages & Verses

Trace the letter Ww. Then write the letter Ww as many times as possible.

W w Wages

Trace and Write: Bible Passages & Verses

Trace the letter Ww. Then write the letter Ww as many times as possible.

Ww   Weaving

Trace the letter Xx. Then write the letter Xx as many times as possible.

Trace and Write: Bible Passages & Verses

Trace the letter Xx. Then write the letter Xx as many times as possible.

Trace the letter Xx. Then write the letter Xx as many times as possible.

Trace the letter Yy. Then write the letter Yy as many times as possible.

Yy Year

Trace the letter Yy. Then write the letter Yy as many times as possible.

Yy Yoke

Trace and Write: Bible Passages & Verses

Trace the letter Yy. Then write the letter Yy as many times as possible.

Yy Yarn

Trace and Write: Bible Passages & Verses

Trace the letter Zz. Then write the letter Zz as many times as possible.

Zz Zephaniah

Trace and Write: Bible Passages & Verses

Trace the letter Zz. Then write the letter Zz as many times as possible.

Z z Zeal

Trace the letter Zz. Then write the letter Zz as many times as possible.

Zz   Zarephath

Made in the USA
Las Vegas, NV
13 October 2023

79062507R00066